Plant Based Breakfast Cookbook

Quick And Budget Friendly Ideas For Your Plant Based Breakfast and Smoothies Recipes

Jennifer Smith

Table of Contents

RECIPES

Italian Herb Rolls

Servings: 6

Preparation time: 10 minutes

Nutrition (per serving

Calories: 257 kcal

Carbs: 16.6g

Fat: 18.6g

Protein: 5.8g

Fiber: 11.7g

Sugar: 1.5g

Ingredients:

- 1 ¼ cups coconut flour
- ¾ tsp. baking soda
- 6 tbsp. melted coconut oil
- 3 tbsp. Italian seasoning (If you don't have this, you can just use 2/3 tsp. each of: basil, garlic powder, thyme, oregano and onion powder
- 2 flax eggs
- ¾ tsp. salt

Total number of ingredients: 6

Directions:

1. Preheat oven to 300 °F.

2. Add coconut flour, oil, baking soda, and flax eggs to a bowl.
3. Mix well.
4. Add Italian seasoning (or herbs if you don't have this seasoningand salt to the mix.
5. Using your hands, mold the dough, small handfuls at a time, to make mini rolls. You should have about 6 rolls when done.
6. Place on a greased baking sheet.
7. Bake at 300 °F for about 45 minutes.
8. Remove from oven and cool at room temperature.

TIP:

1. The bread is naturally a bit crumbly, but if you don't let it cool for an extended period of time, it will completely fall apart.
2. These lovely rolls are sure to satisfy cravings for carbs and make a delectable side roll to any balanced meal, whether it be a salad, soup, or even as a snack with a drizzle of olive oil.

Tortilla Wraps

Servings: 6

Preparation time: 10 minutes

Nutrition (per serving

Calories: 157 kcal

Carbs: 4.2g

Fat: 13.8g

Protein: 5.0g

Fiber: 1.9g

Sugar: 1.5g

Ingredients:

- ¼ cup ground flaxseed
- ¼ cup hot water
- 1 cup almond flour
- ¼ tsp. baking powder
- ½ tsp. salt

Total number of ingredients: 5

Directions:

1. Mix ground flaxseed with hot water until you get a gel-like substance.
2. In a separate bowl, mix almond flour, salt and baking powder.
3. Add ground flaxseed mixture to almond flour

mixture.

4. Mix thoroughly.

5. Add hot water as needed in order to achieve a perfect dough-like consistency.

6. Knead dough, then separate dough into about 6 balls.

7. Flatten each ball as thinly as possible.

8. Grease a pan.

9. Place each tortilla on greased pan and bake each tortilla until brown on both sides.

10.   Remove pan from oven.

11.   Let cool completely before using as they are easier to mold and fold once cool.

12.   This bread-based recipe comes in handy if you're craving a good old tofu wrap or even a vegan-styled quesadilla!

TIP: Psyllium husk and flaxseed mixed with hot water allows for a gel-like substance to form, which is extremely convenient for achieving a dough-type consistency.

Keto-Vegan Pizza Crust

Servings: 2

Preparation time: 10 minutes

Nutrition (1 Crust Slice

Calories: 134 kcal

Carbs: 3.4g

Fat: 11.8g

Protein: 4.9g

Fiber: 6.3g

Sugar: 1.6g

Ingredients:

- 1 tsp. salt
- 1 tbsp. olive oil
- 1 cup warm water
- 2 ½ tsp. active yeast
- 3 cups almond flour
- 1 pinch dried oregano, ground
- 1 pinch dried basil leaf

Total number of ingredients: 7

Directions:

1. Preheat oven to 300 °F.
2. Place warm water in a cup (Note: It must be the right temperature or it will not work).

3. Add yeast to cup.
4. Stir for one minute until you see a light brown mixture.
5. Let sit for 5 minutes until a thin layer of foam forms on top.
6. In a separate bowl, add almond flour and salt.
7. Mix almond flour and salt. Once done mixing, form a well in the middle of the almond flour-salt mixture.
8. Pour yeast mixture and olive oil into well center and begin mixing ingredients.
9. Mix until a dough is achieved. Add more or less flour depending on consistency of dough.
10.   Separate into 2 balls.
11.   Using a rolling pin, flatten balls into circles of dough.
12.   Place dough in oven and allow to Cooking Time: halfway for about 6 minutes.
13.   Take out dough.
14.   Place pizza toppings on dough.
15.   Place pizza dough back in oven to finish baking for 3-6 minutes.
16.   Once baked, remove from oven.

17.   Let cool for 2 minutes, then use a pizza slicer to slice into 8 pieces per pizza.

This adapted ketogenic vegan pizza crust is the perfect substitute if you're looking for a quick pizza without the excess carbs. This crust works best as thin to regular crust, but not deep dish. Pair with some fresh tomato sauce, vegan cashew-parmesan cheese, mushrooms, spinach, or even tofu if you like!

Coconut & Seeds Granola

Preparation time: 10 minutes

Cooking time: 20 minutes

Servings: 15

Ingredients:

- 3 cups unsweetened coconut flakes
- 1 cup walnuts, chopped
- ½ cup flaxseeds
- 2/3 cup pumpkin seeds
- 2/3 cup sunflower seeds
- ¼ cup coconut oil, melted
- 1 teaspoon ground ginger
- 1 teaspoon ground cinnamon
- 1/8 teaspoon ground cloves
- 1/8 teaspoon ground cardamom
- Pinch of salt

Directions:

1. Preheat the oven to 350 degrees F. Lightly, grease a large rimmed baking sheet.
2. In a bowl, add the coconut flakes, walnuts, flaxseeds, pumpkin seeds, sunflower seeds, coconut oil, spices and salt and toss to coat well.

3. Transfer the mixture onto the prepared baking sheet and spread in an even layer.
4. Bake for about 20 minutes, stirring after every 3-4 minutes.
5. Remove the baking sheet from the oven and let the granola cool completely before serving.
6. Break the granola into desired sized chunks and serve with your favorite non-dairy milk.

Meal Preparation time: Tip:

Transfer granola in an airtight container and store in a cool, dry place for up to 2 weeks.

Nutrition:

Calories: 292, Fats: 26.4g, Carbs: 8.4g, Fiber: 5.3g, Sugar: 1.9g, Proteins: 6.2g, Sodium: 22mg

Panini Flat Bread

Servings: 10

Preparation time: 10 minutes

Nutrition (2 half slices/one sandwich

Calories: 280 kcal

Carbs: 8.1g

Fat: 24.4g

Protein: 8.5g

Fiber: 3.7g

Sugar: 3.1g

Ingredients:

- 3 cups almond flour
- 4 flax eggs
- ⅓ cup coconut flour
- 1 tsp. baking soda
- ½ tsp. garlic powder
- ¼ cup water
- ¼ cup olive oil

Total number of ingredients: 7

Directions:

1. Preheat oven to 350 °F.
2. Mix dry ingredients (coconut flour, almond flour, garlic powder and baking sodatogether

in a bowl.

3. To this bowl, add in flax eggs, olive oil, and water, and mix completely until a dough forms (add extra flour or water accordingly; it should be a bit sticky!).

4. Place dough onto a parchment paper-covered tray and mold into a rough rectangular loaf shape.

5. Place 1 piece of parchment paper on top of loaf.

6. Place loaf in oven and bake for 15-20 minutes until firm.

7. Remove loaf from oven.

8. Remove top piece of parchment paper and let loaf cool completely.

9. Once cool, cut into about 10 square pieces, then cut each piece in half.

Herb Cracker Crisps

Servings: 20

Preparation time: 5 minutes

Nutrition (about 4 crackers

Calories: 201 kcal

Carbs: 4.7g

Fat: 18.4g

Protein: 5.5g

Fiber: 0.4g

Sugar: 1.8g

Ingredients:

- 1 cup almond flour
- 2 flax eggs
- 2 tbsp. canola oil
- 2 tbsp. water
- 1 tbsp. rosemary (can be fresh or dried, but freshly chopped rosemary is preferable as it will give a beautiful, strong taste!
- ½ tsp. garlic powder
- ¼ tsp. dried oregano, ground
- ¼ tsp. dried basil leaf
- ¼ tsp. salt
- 1 pinch black pepper

Total number of ingredients: 10

Directions:

1. Preheat oven to 350 °F.
2. Place all ingredients in a bowl and mix well.
3. Line a pan with non-stick parchment paper.
4. Taking the dough formed in step 2, scoop ½ tbsp. of dough and place on pan. Flatten with your finger to make it as thin as a cracker.
5. Bake for about 5-10 minutes until the outsides are crisp and the insides are just the slightest bit soft (they'll harden even more when cooling).
6. Remove from oven, and let cool.
7. Eat these lovely crisps alone or with a spread to please any cracker-snack cravings you may be having. The infusion of herbs is sure to hit your taste buds and leave you satisfied, with only 4.7g of carbs and 1.8g of sugar per serving!

Berry Beet Velvet Smoothie

Preparation Time: 5 minutes

Cooking Time: 0 minute

Servings: 1

Ingredients:

- 1/2 of frozen banana
- 1 cup mixed red berries
- 1 Medjool date, pitted
- 1 small beet, peeled, chopped
- 1 tablespoon cacao powder
- 1 teaspoon chia seeds
- 1/4 teaspoon vanilla extract, unsweetened
- 1/2 teaspoon lemon juice
- 2 teaspoons coconut butter
- 1 cup coconut milk, unsweetened

Directions:

1. Place all the ingredients in the order in a food processor or blender and then pulse for 2 to 3 minutes at high speed until smooth.
2. Pour the smoothie into a glass and then serve.

Nutrition:

Calories: 234 Cal

Fat: 5 g

Carbs: 42 g

Protein: 11 g

Fiber: 7 g

Tofu & Mushroom Muffins

Preparation time: 20 minutes

Cooking time: 20 minutes

Servings: 6

Ingredients:

- 1 teaspoon olive oil
- 1½ cups fresh mushrooms, chopped
- 1 scallion, chopped
- 1 teaspoon garlic, minced
- 1 teaspoon fresh rosemary, minced
- Ground black pepper, as required
- 1 (12.3-ouncepackage lite firm silken tofu, drained
- ¼ cup unsweetened almond milk
- 2 tablespoons nutritional yeast
- 1 tablespoon arrowroot starch
- 1 teaspoon coconut oil, softened
- ¼ teaspoon ground turmeric

Directions:

1. Preheat the oven to 375 degrees F. Grease a 12 cups of a muffin pan.
2. In a nonstick skillet, heat the oil over medium heat and sauté the scallion and garlic for

about 1 minute.

3. Add the mushrooms and sauté for about 5-7 minutes.

4. Stir in the rosemary and black pepper and remove from the heat.

5. Set aside to cool slightly.

6. In a food processor, add the tofu and remaining ingredients and pulse until smooth.

7. Transfer the tofu mixture into a large bowl.

8. Fold in the mushroom mixture.

9. Place the mixture into prepared muffin cups evenly.

10. Bake for about 20-22 minutes or until a toothpick inserted in the center comes out clean.

11. Remove the muffin pan from the oven and place onto a wire rack to cool for about 10 minutes.

12. Carefully, invert the muffins onto wire rack and serve warm.

Meal Preparation time: Tip:

1. Carefully invert the muffins onto a wire rack to cool completely.

2. Line 1-2 airtight containers with paper towels.
3. Arrange muffins over paper towel in a single layer.
4. Cover the muffins with another paper towel.
5. Refrigerate for about 2-3 days.
6. Reheat in the microwave on High for about 2 minutes before serving.

Nutrition:

Calories: 74, Fats: 3.5g, Carbs: 5.3g, Fiber: 1.4g, Sugar: 1.1g, Proteins: 6.2g, Sodium: 32mg

Dried Fruits And Nuts Breakfast Bread

Servings: 15

Preparation time: 15 minutes

Nutrition (per serving

Calories: 315 kcal

Carbs: 21.1g

Fat: 19.4g

Protein: 6.1g

Fiber: 3.6g

Sugar: 15.1g

Ingredients:

- 2 cups almond flour
- 1 medium banana
- 2 flax eggs
- ¼ cup coconut oil
- 2 tbsp. whole flax seeds
- ¼ tsp. salt
- ½ tsp. baking soda
- 1 ½ cups roughly chopped dried mixed fruit (e.g., cranberries, strawberries, pineapple, cherries
- 1 ½ cups roughly chopped dried nuts (e.g., pecans, almonds, walnuts

Total number of ingredients: 10

Directions:

1. Preheat oven to 300 °F.
2. Lightly grease a loaf pan with olive oil.
3. Place bananas in a bowl, and mash extremely well.
4. To the mashed bananas, add coconut oil and flax eggs.
5. Mix well.
6. Add in flour, baking powder, and salt to the mixture, and mix thoroughly.
7. Top with fruits, nuts, and seeds, and mix until everything is evenly mixed.
8. Pour batter in greased loaf pan, and let bake for about 45 minutes or until knife comes out of the center clean.
9. Remove pan from oven, and let cool completely before slicing.

Note:

1. This bread does not rise, so no worries if you don't see that happening!
2. You will realize how many nutrients you are getting when you eat a slice, as well as how

satisfied and strengthened you feel! Due to the amount of dried fruits and nuts in the recipe, as well as the density of the loaf, one to two slices is more than enough to get you energized and full until lunch time. You can even grab a slice if you're looking for a boost in between your meals.

3. The great thing about this recipe is that it is very adaptable. You can choose whatever assortments of dried fruits or nuts you want to add to the recipe.

Banana Bread

Servings: 13

Preparation time: 5 minutes

Nutrition (per serving

Calories: 106 kcal

Carbs: 12.1g

Fat: 17.9g

Protein: 5.3g

Fiber: 2.3g

Sugar: 5.2g

Ingredients:

- 4 bananas
- 4 flax eggs
- 2 ½ cups almond flour
- ⅓ cup olive oil
- ½ tbsp. baking soda

Total number of ingredients: 5

Directions:

1. Preheat oven to 350 °F.
2. Slightly grease a loaf pan.
3. Chop bananas in quarter inch circular slices.
4. Place chopped bananas in a bowl.
5. Add flax eggs, almond flour, olive oil, and

baking soda to bowl.

6. Mix with spoon until well blended.

7. Pour mixture into loaf pan.

8. Bake for one hour.

9. Remove from oven, and let cool at room temperature.

People on a ketogenic diet usually steer clear of eating bananas due to their high carb content (around 27g for an average sized banana). While this number seems scary, this recipe allows you to satisfy your banana sweet tooth while cutting the carb consumption per piece to about 12g.

Seed And Nut Topped Loaf

Servings: 15

Preparation time: 15 minutes

Nutrition (per serving

Calories: 172 kcal

Carbs: 8.1g

Fat: 13.2g

Protein: 6.1g

Fiber: 3.5g

Sugar: 2.4

Ingredients:

- 2 cups almond flour
- 2 tbsp. coconut flour
- ⅓ cup coconut oil
- ½ cup whole almonds
- 3 tbsp. sesame seeds
- ½ cup pumpkin seeds
- ¼ cup whole flax seeds
- ½ tsp. salt
- 3 flax eggs
- 1 ½ tsp. baking soda
- ¾ cup almond milk
- 3 drops stevia sweetener

- 1 tbsp. apple cider vinegar

Total number of ingredients: 13

Directions:

1. Preheat oven to 350 °F.
2. Blend almonds in a blender until fine.
3. Add flax seeds, sesame seeds, and pumpkin seeds and blend.
4. Add almond flour, coconut flour, salt, and baking soda and blend.
5. In a separate bowl, add flax eggs, coconut oil, almond milk, vinegar, and sweetener. Stir well.
6. Add almond mixture to flax egg mixture and let sit for a few minutes.
7. Grease a loaf pan.
8. Pour batter in pan.
9. Sprinkle left over seeds atop batter (pumpkin, flax, and sesame seeds).
10. Bake for about 45 minutes, or until a knife comes clean out of the middle.
11. Remove from oven, and let cool completely before slicing.
12. This loaf recipe is a dry, nutty spin on a

regular bread loaf. What makes it even better is its low-carb, high-fat content, allowing you to consume a few pieces guilt free.

Low Carb Corn Bread

Servings: 18

Preparation time: 10 minutes

Nutrition (per serving

Calories: 138 kcal

Carbs: 7.2g

Fat: 10.7g

Protein: 3.5g

Fiber: 1.2g

Sugar: 2.6g

Ingredients:

- 2 cups almond flour
- 6 drops stevia sweetener
- 1 tsp. salt
- 2 flax eggs
- 3 ½ tsp. baking powder
- ½ cup vanilla flavored almond milk
- ⅓ cup coconut oil
- 15 oz. can baby corn, finely chopped

Total number of ingredients: 8

Directions:

1. Preheat oven to 350 °F.
2. In a bowl, mix almond flour, salt, and baking

powder.

3. Add stevia, chopped corn, flax eggs, almond milk, and coconut oil.
4. Mix well, ensuring no clumps.
5. Lightly grease a pan.
6. Pour batter in pan.
7. Place pan in oven and let bake 50-60 minutes or until knife comes cleanly out of the middle.

Note:

You would think that people on a ketogenic diet would need to steer clear of corn, but here's a recipe that has been tweaked to prove otherwise! The stevia acts as a natural sweetener with almond meal acting as a substitute for high carb flour options. You can eat a slice for breakfast or in between meals to satisfy cravings.

Mini Italian Toast Crackers

Servings: 13

Preparation time: 5 minutes

Nutrition (about 4 crackers

Calories: 225 kcal

Carbs: 5.4g

Fat: 20.9g

Protein: 6.2g

Fiber: 0.5g

Sugar: 1g

Ingredients:

- 1 ¼ cups almond flour
- 1 flax egg
- 2 tbsp. olive oil
- ¾ tsp. salt
- 1 ½ tbsp. Italian seasoning (or ¼ tsp. each of: basil, garlic powder, thyme, oregano and onion powder).

Total number of ingredients: 5

Directions:

1. Preheat oven to 300 °F.
2. Place all ingredients into a bowl.
3. Mix ingredients into a dough-like consistency.

4. Once dough is formed, place on a cutting board.
5. Shape dough into a thin, long, rectangular prism.
6. Using a knife, cut dough into thin pieces of your liking.
7. Lightly grease a baking tray.
8. Place cut dough on baking tray.
9. Bake for 10 minutes or until crisp.

These Italian crackers are sure to hit that savory spot with the Italian herbs adding a twist to your everyday cracker! Use these as crackers when you're craving a quick, crispy snack, or munch on them in the morning, spreading avocado on them to make a quick breakfast.

Raspberry Lime Smoothie

Preparation time: 5 minutes

Servings 2

Ingredients:

- 1 cup water
- 1 cup fresh or frozen raspberries
- 1 large frozen banana
- 2 tbsp fresh juice, lime
- 1 tsp oil, coconut
- 1 tsp agave

Directions:

1. In a blender put all ingredients and blend until smooth.
2. Take out and serve

Nutrition:

Calories 227,Total Fat 4g, Saturated Fat 1.3g, Cholesterol 0mg, Sodium 7mg, Total Carbohydrate 47.8g, Dietary Fiber 6g, Total Sugars 40.7g, Protein 0.9g, Vitamin D 0mcg, Calcium 22mg, Iron 1mg, Potassium 144mg

Low Carb Sub Bread

Servings: 4 mini subs

Preparation time: 5 minutes

Nutrition (per serving

Calories: 292 kcal

Carbs: 13.3g

Fat: 23.2g

Protein: 9.9g

Fiber 2,5g

Sugar: 3.2g

Ingredients:

- 1 ½ cups almond flour
- 5 tbsp. psyllium husk powder, finely ground
- 2 tsp. baking powder
- 1 tsp. salt
- 2 ½ tbsp. apple cider vinegar
- 2 flax eggs
- 1 cup boiling water

Total number of ingredients: 7

Directions:

1. Preheat oven to 350 °F.
2. In a bowl, mix together almond flour, psyllium husk powder, baking powder, and salt.

3. Add flax eggs and apple cider vinegar and mix well until a dough forms.
4. Add boiling water and continue mixing.
5. Mold dough into 4 mini subs or one large sub (remember the dough should and will rise).
6. Place dough on a slightly greased baking pan. Bake for 45 minutes or until firm.

Yes, while 13.3g carbs may seem like a lot, it must be taken in comparison to a traditional sub sandwich's carb levels: a whole 40g. Enjoy this recipe when you find yourself reminiscing on those tasty sub sandwiches, and simply indulge the guilt-free way!

Nuts & Sees Granola

Preparation time: 15 minutes

Cooking time: 28 minutes

Servings: 12

Ingredients:

- ½ cup unsweetened coconut flakes
- 1 cup raw almonds
- 1 cup raw cashews
- ¼ cup raw sunflower seeds, shelled
- ¼ cup raw pumpkin seeds, shelled
- ¼ cup coconut oil
- ½ cup maple syrup
- 1 teaspoon vanilla extract
- ½ cup golden raisins
- ½ cup black raisins
- Salt, as required

Directions:

1. Preheat the oven to 275 degrees F. Line a large baking sheet with parchment paper.
2. In a food processor, add the coconut flakes, almonds, cashews and seeds and pulse until chopped finely.
3. Meanwhile, in a medium nonstick pan, add the

oil, maple syrup and vanilla extract over medium-high heat and Cooking Time: for about 3 minutes, stirring continuously.

4. Remove from the heat and immediately stir in the nuts mixture.
5. Transfer the mixture into the prepared baking sheet and spread evenly.
6. Bake for about 25 minutes, stirring twice.
7. Remove from the oven and immediately stir in the raisins.
8. Sprinkle with a little salt.
9. With the back of a spatula, flatten the surface of mixture.
10. Set aside to cool completely.
11. Then break into desired size chunks and serve with your choice of non-dairy milk and fruit's topping.

Meal Preparation time: Tip:

Transfer granola in an airtight container and store in a cool, dry place for up to 2 weeks.

Nutrition:

Calories: 237, Fats: 18.4g, Carbs: 25.5g, Fiber: 2.6g, Sugar: 16.3g, Proteins: 5g, Sodium: 18mg

Plain Loaf

Servings: 15

Preparation time: 5 minutes

Nutrition (per serving

Calories: 142 kcal

Carbs: 13.4g

Fat: 43.1g

Protein: 3.9g

Fiber: 3,5g

Sugar: 1.5g

Ingredients:

- 1 cup coconut flour
- 6 cups almond flour
- ¼ cup flax seed
- 5 flax eggs
- ½ cup water
- ½ cup MCT oil
- 3 tsp. baking powder
- 1 tsp. salt
- 1 tbsp. apple cider vinegar

Total number of ingredients: 8

Directions:

1. Preheat oven to 350 °F.

2. In a bowl, mix together dry ingredients: almond flour, coconut flour, baking powder, salt, and flax seeds.

3. In a separate bowl, mix together coconut oil, water and apple cider vinegar.

4. Combine dry and liquid ingredients from Steps 2 and Mix well.

5. Pour batter in a slightly greased large loaf pan.

6. Bake for 30-45 minutes or until firm.

Note: Make sure the loaf is completely cooled before slicing it.

Here is another spin on a plain bread type loaf that you could use a spread on, or for on-the-go sandwiches!

2-Minute Microwave Burger Bun

Servings: 1

Preparation time: 3 minutes

Nutrition (1 bun

Calories: 280 kcal

Carbs: 10g

Fat: 23.9g

Protein: 9.5g

Fiber: 4.4g

Sugar: 1.4g

Ingredients:

- ⅓ cup almond flour (or any other nut flour of your choice
- 1 flax egg
- ½ tsp. baking powder
- ½ tsp. cocoa powder
- ¼ tsp. salt
- ¾ tsp. sesame seeds

Total number of ingredients: 6

Directions:

1. In a bowl, add the almond flour, baking powder, cocoa powder, and salt. Mix thoroughly, or you will end up tasting weird

bits of baking powder, salt, or cocoa in your burger bun!

2. Add the flax egg to mixture and stir until well blended.

3. Slightly grease a cup large enough to fit the batter.

4. Sprinkle some of the sesame seeds at the bottom of the cup.

5. Pour batter on top of the seeds.

6. Sprinkle the rest of the seeds on top of the batter.

7. Place cup in microwave.

8. Microwave for about 2 minutes or until firm.

Sounds too easy to be true, right? Not to mention it makes the perfect complement to the perfect ketogenic vegan burger. This bun would be great with a seasoned tofu patty, grilled mushrooms, and crisp, fresh veggies like tomato and lettuce.

Creamy Chocolate Shake

Preparation time: 10 minutes

Servings 2

Ingredients:

- 2 frozen ripe bananas, chopped
- 1/3 cup frozen strawberries
- 2 tbsp cocoa powder
- 2 tbsp salted almond butter
- 2 cups unsweetened vanilla almond milk
- 1 dash Stevia or agave nectar
- 1/3 cup ice

Directions:

1. Add all ingredients in a blender and blend until smooth.
2. Take out and serve.

Nutrition:

Calories 272, Total Fat 14.3g, Saturated Fat 1.5g, Cholesterol 0mg, Sodium 315mg, Total Carbohydrate 37g, Dietary Fiber 7.3g, Total Sugars 16.8g, Protein 6.2g, Vitamin D 2mcg, Calcium 735mg, Iron 2mg, Potassium 732mg

Seed-Based Crackers

Servings: 25 crackers

Preparation time: 5 minutes

Nutrition (per serving

Calories: 53 kcal

Carbs: 3.5g

Fat: 3.6g

Protein: 1.6g

Fiber: 1.6g

Sugar: 0.1g

Ingredients:

- 1 cup flaxseed, ground
- 1 cup pumpkin seeds
- ½ cup sesame seeds
- ½ tsp. salt
- 1 cup hot water

Total number of ingredients: 5

Directions:

1. Preheat oven to 300 °F.
2. Place all ingredients in a bowl and mix.
3. Let sit for five minutes (the flaxseed will form a gel with the water).
4. Spread mixture on a parchment paper-lined pan.
5. Using a knife, cut dough evenly into about 25 crackers.
6. Place in oven and bake until firm.
7. Turn oven off, leaving crackers in oven for about 1 hour so that crackers dry out.
8. Simple and quick homemade crackers are sure to satisfy your need of a quick snack, or even to use as a base for a low-carb spread.

The 'Green Machine' Smoothie

Preparation time: 3 minutes

Servings 2

Ingredients

- 1 cup spinach
- ½ cup broccoli
- 2 Sticks of Celery
- 4 tbsp desiccated coconut
- 1 banana
- 1 scoop vegan unflavored protein powder
- 1 cup almond milk
- 1 cupwater

Directions:

1. Pop everything in a blender and blitz
2. Pour into glasses and serve.

Nutrition:

Calories 780, Total Fat 66.5g, Saturated Fat 57.9g, Cholesterol 0mg, Sodium 224mg, Total Carbohydrate 38.8g, Dietary Fiber 15g, Total Sugars 18.4g, Protein 19.6g, Vitamin D 0mcg, Calcium 82mg, Iron 5mg, Potassium 1108mg

Sweet Coffee and Cacao Smoothie

Preparation time: 3 minutes

Servings 2

Ingredients

- 2 tsp Coffee
- ½ a Banana
- 1 cup Almond Milk
- 1 tsp Cashew Butter
- 2 tsp Cacao Powder
- 1 tsp maple Syrup
- 1 scoop vegan protein powder
- ½ cup Chocolate

Directions:

1. Pop everything in a blender and blitz
2. Pour into glasses and serve.

Nutrition:

Calories 614, Total Fat 43.2g, Saturated Fat 34.6g, Cholesterol 10mg, Sodium 146mg, Total Carbohydrate 44.7g, Dietary Fiber 5.4g, Total Sugars 31.2g, Protein 17.6g, Vitamin D 0mcg, Calcium 104mg, Iron 4mg, Potassium 614mg

Amazing Blueberry Smoothie

Preparation time: 5 minutes

Servings 2

Ingredients:

- ½ avocado
- 1 cup frozen blueberries
- 1 cup raw spinach
- ¼ tsp sea salt
- 1 cup soy
- 1 frozen banana

Directions:

1. Blend everything in a powerful blender until you have a smooth, creamy shake.
2. Enjoy your healthy shake and start your morning on a fresh note!

Nutrition:

Calories 269, Total Fat 12.3g, Saturated Fat 2.3g, Cholesterol 0mg, Sodium 312mg, Total Carbohydrate 37.6g, Dietary Fiber 8.2g, Total Sugars 22.9g, Protein 6.4g, Vitamin D 0mcg, Calcium 52mg, Iron 3mg, Potassium 528mg

Go-Green Smoothie

Preparation time: 5 minutes

Servings 1

Ingredients:

- 2 tablespoons, natural cashew butter
- 1 ripe banana
- 2/3 cup, unsweetened coconut
- ½ cup kale

Directions:

1. Put everything inside a powerful blender.
2. Blend until you have a smooth, creamy shake.
3. Enjoy your special green smoothie.

Nutrition:

Calories 500, Total Fat 33.2g, Saturated Fat 18.9g, Cholesterol 0mg, Sodium 161mg, Total Carbohydrate 48.6g, Dietary Fiber 10.4g, Total Sugars 19.8g, Protein 9.1g, Vitamin D 0mcg, Calcium 72mg, Iron 9mg, Potassium 777mg

Hidden Kale Smoothie

Preparation time: 5 minutes

Servings 2

Ingredients:

- 1 medium ripe banana, peeled and sliced
- ½ cup frozen mixed berries
- 1 tbsp hulled hemp seeds
- 2 cups frozen or fresh kale
- 2/3 cup 100% pomegranate juice
- 2¼ cups filtered water

Directions:

1. Add all ingredients in a blender and blend until smooth.
2. Take out and serve.

Nutrition:

Calories 164, Total Fat 2g, Saturated Fat 0.2g, Cholesterol 0mg, Sodium 51mg, Total Carbohydrate 34.2g, Dietary Fiber 3.9g, Total Sugars 17.7g, Protein 4.1g, Vitamin D 0mcg, Calcium 124mg, Iron 2mg, Potassium 776mg

Blueberry Protein Shake

Preparation time: 5 minutes

Servings 1

Ingredients:

- ½ cup cottage cheese
- 3 tbsp vanilla protein powder
- ½ cup frozen blueberries
- ½ tsp maple extract
- ¼ tsp vanilla extract
- 2 tsp flaxseed meal
- Sweetener, choice
- 10-15 ice cubes
- ¼ cup water

Directions:

1. Add all ingredients in a blender and blend until smooth.
2. Take out and serve.

Nutrition:

Calories 559, Total Fat 4.2g, Saturated Fat 1.9g, Cholesterol 14mg, Sodium 659mg, Total Carbohydrate 31.1g, Dietary Fiber 4.5g, Total Sugars 20.7g, Protein 98g, Vitamin D 0mcg,

Calcium 518mg, Iron 3mg, Potassium 676mg

Banana Green Smoothie

Preparation time: 5 minutes

Servings 1

Ingredients:

- 1 cup coconut water
- ¾ cup plant-based milk
- ¼ tsp vanilla extract
- 1 heaping cup loosely packed spinach
- 2-3 cups frozen bananas, sliced

Directions:

Blend everything until smooth and serve.

Nutrition:

Calories 364, Total Fat 4.8g, Saturated Fat 2.6g, Cholesterol 15mg, Sodium 111mg, Total Carbohydrate 78g, Dietary Fiber 8g, Total Sugars 45.1g, Protein 9.6g, Vitamin D 1mcg, Calcium 257mg, Iron 1mg, Potassium 1241mg

Coconut Granola

Preparation time: 10 minutes

Cooking time: 18 minutes

Servings: 4

Ingredients:

- 1 tablespoon coconut oil, melted
- 1 tablespoon coconut butter, melted
- 2-3 tablespoons maple syrup
- 1 teaspoon orange zest, grated freshly
- ½ teaspoon ground cinnamon
- Pinch of sea salt
- 2 cups coconut flakes

Directions:

1. Preheat the oven to 350 degrees F. Line a cookie sheet with parchment paper.
2. In a bowl, mix together all ingredients except coconut flakes.
3. Spread coconut flakes in prepared cookie sheet.
4. Pour coconut oil mixture over flakes and gently, stir to mix.
5. Bake for about 12-15 minutes.
6. Remove from the oven and set aside to cool

completely.

7. Then break into desired size chunks and serve with your choice of non-dairy milk and fruit's topping.

8. Meal Preparation time: Tip:

9. Transfer granola in an airtight container and store in a cool, dry place for up to 2 weeks.

Nutrition:

Calories: 221, Fats: 19g, Carbs: 14g, Fiber: 4.4g, Sugar: 8.7g, Proteins: 1.6g, Sodium: 69mg

2-Minute Microwave Fruit Bread In A Mug!

Servings: 4 slices

Preparation time: 3 minutes

Nutrition (1 circled slice

Calories: 165 kcal

Carbs: 25.5g

Fat: 6.2g

Protein: 4.1g

Fiber: 0.8g

Sugar: 13.3g

Ingredients:

- ⅓ cup almond flour (or any other nut flour of your preference
- 1 flax egg
- ¼ tsp. baking soda
- ¼ tsp. salt
- 2 tbsp. of your desired dried fruit (For this recipe, raspberries and strawberries were chosen

Total number of ingredients: 5

Directions:

1. To a bowl, add almond flour, baking soda, dried fruits, and salt. Mix thoroughly.

2. Add flax egg and stir until evenly distributed. Also make sure dried fruits are evenly distributed in the batter.
3. Lightly grease a mug that is big enough to hold batter.
4. Pour batter into mug and microwave for about 2 minutes.
5. Remove mug from oven, and slice mini loaf into about 4 pieces.
6. This recipe is an adaptation of the new craze of "microwave bread" which   allows you to exhaust minimal effort yet indulge to the maximum.

Raspberries and strawberries are great for those on a ketogenic diet as fresh raspberries contain 3.3g of carbs per ounce and strawberries 2.2g. Ultimately, this recipe is such an efficient, tasty, and filling way to put a spin on your normal loaf of bread.

Almond Pan Loaf

Servings: 15

Preparation time: 10 minutes

Nutrition (per serving

Calories: 381 kcal

Carbs: 9.5g

Fat: 33g

Protein: 11.7g

Fiber: 5.2g

Sugar: 2.0g

Ingredients:

- 6 cups almond flour (or any other nut flour that you prefer
- 3 flax eggs
- ½ cup olive oil
- ¼ cup almond milk (or water, if you want to reduce the caloric content
- 2 tsp. baking powder
- 1 tsp. baking soda
- ¼ tsp. salt

Total number of ingredients: 7

Directions:

1. Preheat oven to 350 °F.

2. Lightly grease a large loaf pan with oil.
3. Combine all ingredients in a bowl, ensuring they are well mixed.
4. Pour mixture into loaf pan and bake for about 1 hour.
5. Remove pan from oven and let cool.
6. Once cooled, remove loaf by flipping pan upside down.
7. Slice evenly.

Note: Though this bread does not rise as much as a "normal" loaf would, per se, its plain taste is the perfect complement to a sandwich on the go! Also, if you decide to use this to make a quick, easy lunch, two slices yield only 3 grams of carbs for your daily count compared to a whopping 22 grams of regular bread!

Hot Pink Smoothie

Preparation Time: 5 minutes

Cooking Time: 0 minute

Servings: 1

Ingredients:

- 1 clementine, peeled, segmented
- 1/2 frozen banana
- 1 small beet, peeled, chopped
- 1/8 teaspoon sea salt
- 1/2 cup raspberries
- 1 tablespoon chia seeds
- 1/4 teaspoon vanilla extract, unsweetened
- 2 tablespoons almond butter
- 1 cup almond milk, unsweetened

Directions:

1. Place all the ingredients in the order in a food processor or blender and then pulse for 2 to 3 minutes at high speed until smooth.
2. Pour the smoothie into a glass and then serve.

Nutrition:

Calories: 278 Cal

Fat: 5.6 g

Carbs: 37.2 g

Protein: 6.2 g

Fiber: 13.2 g

Maca Caramel Frap

Preparation Time: 5 minutes

Cooking Time: 0 minute

Servings: 4

Ingredients:

- 1/2 of frozen banana, sliced
- 1/4 cup cashews, soaked for 4 hours
- 2 Medjool dates, pitted
- 1 teaspoon maca powder
- 1/8 teaspoon sea salt
- 1/2 teaspoon vanilla extract, unsweetened
- 1/4 cup almond milk, unsweetened
- 1/4 cup cold coffee, brewed

Directions:

1. Place all the ingredients in the order in a food processor or blender and then pulse for 2 to 3 minutes at high speed until smooth.
2. Pour the smoothie into a glass and then serve.

Nutrition:

Calories: 450 Cal

Fat: 170 g

Carbs: 64 g

Protein: 7 g

Fiber: 0 g

Peanut Butter Vanilla Green Shake

Preparation Time: 5 minutes

Cooking Time: 0 minute

Servings: 1

Ingredients:

- 1 teaspoon flax seeds
- 1 frozen banana
- 1 cup baby spinach
- 1/8 teaspoon sea salt
- 1/2 teaspoon ground cinnamon
- 1/4 teaspoon vanilla extract, unsweetened
- 2 tablespoons peanut butter, unsweetened
- 1/4 cup ice
- 1 cup coconut milk, unsweetened

Directions:

1. Place all the ingredients in the order in a food processor or blender and then pulse for 2 to 3 minutes at high speed until smooth.
2. Pour the smoothie into a glass and then serve.

Nutrition:

Calories: 298 Cal

Fat: 11 g

Carbs: 32 g

Protein: 24 g

Fiber: 8 g

Peppermint Monster Smoothie

Preparation time: 5 minutes

Servings 1

Ingredients:

- 1 large frozen banana, peeled
- 1½ cups non-dairy milk
- A handful of fresh mint leaves, stems removed
- 1-2 handfuls spinach

Directions:

1. Add all ingredients in a blender and blend until smooth.
2. Take out and serve

Nutrition:

Calories 799, Total Fat 28.1g, Saturated Fat 16.7g, Cholesterol 110mg   , Sodium 645mg, Total Carbohydrate 98.4g, Dietary Fiber 4.5g, Total Sugars 77.2g, Protein 46.2g,   Vitamin D 7mcg, Calcium 1634mg, Iron 2mg, Potassium 1366mg

Green Colada

Preparation Time: 5 minutes

Cooking Time: 0 minute

Servings: 1

Ingredients:

- 1/2 cup frozen pineapple chunks
- 1/2 banana
- 1/2 teaspoon spirulina powder
- 1/4 teaspoon vanilla extract, unsweetened
- 1 cup of coconut milk

Directions:

1. Place all the ingredients in the order in a food processor or blender and then pulse for 2 to 3 minutes at high speed until smooth.
2. Pour the smoothie into a glass and then serve.

Nutrition:

Calories: 127 Cal

Fat: 3 g

Carbs: 25 g

Protein: 3 g

Fiber: 4 g

Chocolate Oat Smoothie

Preparation Time: 5 minutes

Cooking Time: 0 minute

Servings: 1

Ingredients:

- ¼ cup rolled oats
- 1 ½ tablespoon cocoa powder, unsweetened
- 1 teaspoon flax seeds
- 1 large frozen banana
- 1/8 teaspoon sea salt
- 1/8 teaspoon cinnamon
- ¼ teaspoon vanilla extract, unsweetened
- 2 tablespoons almond butter
- 1 cup coconut milk, unsweetened

Directions:

1. Place all the ingredients in the order in a food processor or blender and then pulse for 2 to 3 minutes at high speed until smooth.
2. Pour the smoothie into a glass and then serve.

Nutrition:

Calories: 262 Cal

Fat: 7.3 g

Carbs: 50.4 g

Protein: 8.1 g

Fiber: 9.6 g

Pumpkin Apple Pie Smoothie

Preparation time: 10 minutes

Cooking Time: 5 minutes

Ingredients:

- 2 h
- 1 apple - stripped, cored, and slashed
- 2 tablespoons water, or varying
- 2/3 cup unsweetened vanilla-enhanced almond milk
- 1/4 cup pumpkin puree
- 1/2 teaspoons darker sugar, or to taste
- 1/4 teaspoon pumpkin pie zest
- 2/3 cup squashed ice shapes

Add all fixings to list

Directions:

1. Place apple in a plastic microwave-safe bowl; pour in enough water to cover 1/4-inch of the base of bowl. Halfway spread bowl with a cover or paper towel. Microwave in brief interims until apple is mellowed, 2 to 3 minutes. Freeze apple in a similar holder with water until strong, 2 hours to medium-term.

2. Blend solidified apple, almond milk, and

pumpkin puree in a blender until smooth; include dark colored sugar and pumpkin pie flavor. Mix until smooth. Include ice and mix until smooth.

References

Cook's Note:

Milk with a scramble of vanilla concentrate can be fill in for unsweetened vanilla almond milk if necessary.

Nutrition: 185 calories; 2.2 g fat; 42.6 g carbohydrates;1.8 g protein; 0 mg cholesterol; 261 mg sodium.

Peach Crumble Shake

Preparation Time: 5 minutes

Cooking Time: 0 minute

Servings: 1

Ingredients:

- 1 tablespoon chia seeds
- ¼ cup rolled oats
- 2 peaches, pitted, sliced
- ¾ teaspoon ground cinnamon
- 1 Medjool date, pitted
- ½ teaspoon vanilla extract, unsweetened
- 2 tablespoons lemon juice
- ½ cup of water
- 1 tablespoon coconut butter
- 1 cup coconut milk, unsweetened

Directions:

1. Place all the ingredients in the order in a food processor or blender and then pulse for 2 to 3 minutes at high speed until smooth.
2. Pour the smoothie into a glass and then serve.

Nutrition:

Calories: 270 Cal

Fat: 4 g

Carbs: 28 g

Protein: 25 g

Fiber: 3 g

Wild Ginger Green Smoothie

Preparation Time: 5 minutes

Cooking Time: 0 minute

Servings: 1

Ingredients:

- 1/2 cup pineapple chunks, frozen
- 1/2 cup chopped kale
- 1/2 frozen banana
- 1 tablespoon lime juice
- 2 inches ginger, peeled, chopped
- 1/2 cup coconut milk, unsweetened
- 1/2 cup coconut water

Directions:

1. Place all the ingredients in the order in a food processor or blender and then pulse for 2 to 3 minutes at high speed until smooth.
2. Pour the smoothie into a glass and then serve.

Nutrition:

Calories: 331 Cal

Fat: 14 g

Carbs: 40 g

Protein: 16 g

Fiber: 9 g

Spiced Strawberry Smoothie

Preparation Time: 5 minutes

Cooking Time: 0 minute

Servings: 1

Ingredients:

- 1 tablespoon goji berries, soaked
- 1 cup strawberries
- 1/8 teaspoon sea salt
- 1 frozen banana
- 1 Medjool date, pitted
- 1 scoop vanilla-flavored whey protein
- 2 tablespoons lemon juice
- ¼ teaspoon ground ginger
- ½ teaspoon ground cinnamon
- 1 tablespoon almond butter
- 1 cup almond milk, unsweetened

Directions:

1. Place all the ingredients in the order in a food processor or blender and then pulse for 2 to 3 minutes at high speed until smooth.
2. Pour the smoothie into a glass and then serve.

Nutrition:

Calories: 182 Cal

Fat: 1.3 g

Carbs: 34 g

Protein: 6.4 g

Fiber: 0.7 g

Seed-Based Herb Crackers

Servings: 16

Preparation time: 50 minutes

Nutrition (per serving

Calories: 190 kcal

Carbs: 5.5g

Fat: 14.7g

Protein: 9.0g

Fiber: 5.3g

Sugar: 0.3g

Ingredients:

- 2 cups ground flaxseed
- 2 cups ground hemp seed
- 2 cups warm water
- 1 tsp. salt
- 1 tsp. black pepper
- Italian herbs or other herbs to taste

Total number of ingredients: 6

Directions:

1. Preheat oven to 350°F.
2. Line your baking plate with parchment paper.
3. Combine flax seeds, hemp seeds, salt, and herbs in mixing bowl and stir thoroughly.

4. Pour in water and stir.

5. Let mixture sit for 5 minutes until water is absorbed.

6. Spread out mixture evenly on the baking plate, about 1/8 inch thick.

7. Divide into 16 pieces without damaging parchment paper.

8. Bake for 50 minutes.

9. Remove from oven and cool down.

10.   Break into 16 pieces for serving.

11.   Can be stored up to a week or frozen.

12.   Check out this delicious keto friendly cracker recipe that is suitable for ketogenic vegans and is extremely simple to make!

Banana Bread Shake With Walnut Milk

Preparation Time: 5 minutes

Cooking Time: 0 minute

Servings: 2

Ingredients:

- 2 cups sliced frozen bananas
- 3 cups walnut milk
- 1/8 teaspoon grated nutmeg
- 1 tablespoon maple syrup
- 1 teaspoon ground cinnamon
- 1/2 teaspoon vanilla extract, unsweetened
- 2 tablespoons cacao nibs

Directions:

1. Place all the ingredients in the order in a food processor or blender and then pulse for 2 to 3 minutes at high speed until smooth.
2. Pour the smoothie into two glasses and then serve.

Nutrition:

Calories: 339.8 Cal

Fat: 19 g

Carbs: 39 g

Protein: 4.3 g

Fiber: 1 g

Double Chocolate Hazelnut Espresso Shake

Preparation Time: 5 minutes

Cooking Time: 0 minute

Servings: 1

Ingredients:

- 1 frozen banana, sliced
- 1/4 cup roasted hazelnuts
- 4 Medjool dates, pitted, soaked
- 2 tablespoons cacao nibs, unsweetened
- 1 1/2 tablespoons cacao powder, unsweetened
- 1/8 teaspoon sea salt
- 1 teaspoon vanilla extract, unsweetened
- 1 cup almond milk, unsweetened
- 1/2 cup ice
- 4 ounces espresso, chilled

Directions:

1. Place all the ingredients in the order in a food processor or blender and then pulse for 2 to 3 minutes at high speed until smooth.

2. Pour the smoothie into a glass and then serve.

Nutrition:

Calories: 210 Cal

Fat: 5 g

Carbs: 27 g

Protein: 16.8 g

Fiber: 0.2 g

Green Smoothie Bowl

Preparation time: 10 minutes

"Smoothie in a bowl, ideal for a fast and sound breakfast."

Ingredients:

Smoothie:

- 3 cups new spinach
- 1 banana
- 1/2 (14 ouncewould coconut be able to drain
- 1/2 cup solidified mango pieces
- 1/2 cup coconut water

Toppings:

- 1/3 cup new raspberries
- 1/4 cup new blueberries
- 2 tablespoons granola
- 1 tablespoon coconut chips
- 1/4 teaspoon cut almonds
- 1/4 teaspoon chia seeds (discretionary

Add all fixings to list

Bearings

Blend spinach, banana, coconut milk, mango, and coconut water in a blender until smooth. Empty smoothie into a bowl and top with raspberries, blueberries, granola, coconut chips, almonds, and chia seeds.

References

Cook's Note:

For thicker smoothie, include cut solidified banana.
Nutrition: 374 calories; 25.6 g fat; 37 g carbohydrates;6.3 g protein; 0 mg cholesterol; 116 mg sodium.

Strawberry, Banana And Coconut Shake

Preparation Time: 5 minutes

Cooking Time: 0 minute

Servings: 1

Ingredients:

- 1 tablespoon coconut flakes
- 1 1/2 cups frozen banana slices
- 8 strawberries, sliced
- 1/2 cup coconut milk, unsweetened
- 1/4 cup strawberries for topping

Directions:

1. Place all the ingredients in the order in a food processor or blender, except for topping and then pulse for 2 to 3 minutes at high speed until smooth.
2. Pour the smoothie into a glass and then serve.

Nutrition:

Calories: 335 Cal

Fat: 5 g

Carbs: 75 g

Protein: 4 g

Fiber: 9 g

Tropical Vibes Green Smoothie

Preparation Time: 5 minutes

Cooking Time: 0 minute

Servings: 1

Ingredients:

- 2 stalks of kale, ripped
- 1 frozen banana
- 1 mango, peeled, pitted, chopped
- 1/8 teaspoon sea salt
- ¼ cup of coconut yogurt
- ½ teaspoon vanilla extract, unsweetened
- 1 tablespoon ginger juice
- ½ cup of orange juice
- ½ cup of coconut water

Directions:

1. Place all the ingredients in the order in a food processor or blender and then pulse for 2 to 3 minutes at high speed until smooth.
2. Pour the smoothie into a glass and then serve.

Nutrition:

Calories: 197.5 Cal

Fat: 1.3 g

Carbs: 30 g

Protein: 16.3 g

Fiber: 4.8 g

Acai Smoothie Bowl

Preparation time: 10 minutes

Ingredients:

On

- 1 huge banana, isolated
- 3 1/2 ounces acai berry mash, solidified, unsweetened
- 2 tablespoons soy milk, or more varying
- 2 tablespoons granola
- Add all fixings to list

Bearings

1. Combine acai mash, 2/3 of the banana, and 2 tablespoons of soy milk in a blender; mix until smooth, yet at the same time thick. Include more soy milk varying; smoothie ought to have the consistency of solidified yogurt.
2. Slice the rest of the banana. Empty thick smoothie into a bowl and top with granola and cut bananas.

Sustenance Facts

Nutrition: 282 calories; 9.6 g fat; 45.1 g carbohydrates;4.8 g protein; 0 mg cholesterol; 46 mg sodium.

Two-Ingredient Banana Pancakes

Preparation time: 3 minutes

Cooking Time: 2 minutes

Ingredients:

- 5 min., 1 servings, 78 cals
- 1 ready banana
- 1 egg
- 1/2 teaspoon vanilla concentrate (discretionary
- Add all fixings to list

Bearings

1. Include a notePrint
2. Mix banana and egg together in a bowl until no bumps remain. Add vanilla concentrate to the hitter.
3. Heat a lubed skillet or frying pan over medium warmth. Empty hitter into the dish. Cooking Time: until bubbles show up, around 1 moment. Flip and Cooking Time: until brilliant, around brief more.

Nutrition: 78 calories; 5 g fat; 0.7 g starches; 6.3 g protein; 186 mg cholesterol; 70 mg sodium.

Orange Chia Smoothie

Preparation time: 10 minutes

Ingredients:

- 1 little orange, stripped
- 1/2 cup solidified mango pieces
- 1 tablespoon cashew spread
- 1 tablespoon unsweetened coconut pieces
- 1 teaspoon chia seeds
- 1 teaspoon ground flax seeds
- 1/2 cup squeezed orange
- water varying (discretionary

Add all fixings to list

Bearings

Layer orange, mango, cashew spread, coconut, chia seeds, and flax into a blender; include squeezed orange. Spread and mix blend until smooth, including water for a more slender smoothie.

Nutrition: 313 calories; 14.1 g fat; 45.8 g starches; 6.3 g protein; 0 mg cholesterol; 112 mg sodium.

Peanut Butter And Mocha Smoothie

Preparation Time: 5 minutes

Cooking Time: 0 minute

Servings: 1

Ingredients:

- 1 frozen banana, chopped
- 1 scoop of chocolate protein powder
- 2 tablespoons rolled oats
- 1/8 teaspoon sea salt
- ¼ teaspoon vanilla extract, unsweetened
- 1 teaspoon cocoa powder, unsweetened
- 2 tablespoons peanut butter
- 1 shot of espresso
- ½ cup almond milk, unsweetened

Directions:

1. Place all the ingredients in the order in a food processor or blender and then pulse for 2 to 3 minutes at high speed until smooth.
2. Pour the smoothie into a glass and then serve.

Nutrition:

Calories: 380 Cal

Fat: 14 g

Carbs: 29 g

Protein: 38 g

Fiber: 4 g

Mango Craze Juice Blend

Preparation time: 5 minutes

Ingredients:

- 5 min., 4 servings, 150 cals
- 3 cups diced mango
- 1/2 cups hacked crisp or solidified peaches
- 1/4 cup hacked orange portions
- 1/4 cup hacked and pitted nectarine
- 1/2 cup squeezed orange
- 2 cups ice

Add all fixings to list

Bearings

Place mango, peaches, orange, nectarine, squeezed orange, and ice into a blender. Mix for 1 moment, or until smooth.

Nutrition: 150 calories; 0.6 g fat; 38.4 g carbohydrates;1.3 g protein; 0 mg cholesterol; 9 mg sodium.

Tahini Shake With Cinnamon And Lime

Preparation Time: 5 minutes

Cooking Time: 0 minute

Servings: 1

Ingredients:

- 1 frozen banana
- 2 tablespoons tahini
- 1/8 teaspoon sea salt
- ¾ teaspoon ground cinnamon
- ¼ teaspoon vanilla extract, unsweetened
- 2 teaspoons lime juice
- 1 cup almond milk, unsweetened

Directions:

1. Place all the ingredients in the order in a food processor or blender and then pulse for 2 to 3 minutes at high speed until smooth.
2. Pour the smoothie into a glass and then serve.

Nutrition:

Calories: 225 Cal

Fat: 15 g

Carbs: 22 g

Protein: 6 g

Fiber: 8 g

Ginger And Greens Smoothie

Preparation Time: 5 minutes

Cooking Time: 0 minute

Servings: 1

Ingredients:

- 1 frozen banana
- 2 cups baby spinach
- 2-inch piece of ginger, peeled, chopped
- ¼ teaspoon cinnamon
- ¼ teaspoon vanilla extract, unsweetened
- 1/8 teaspoon salt
- 1 scoop vanilla protein powder
- 1/8 teaspoon cayenne pepper
- 2 tablespoons lemon juice
- 1 cup of orange juice

Directions:

1. Place all the ingredients in the order in a food processor or blender and then pulse for 2 to 3 minutes at high speed until smooth.
2. Pour the smoothie into a glass and then serve.

Nutrition:

Calories: 320 Cal

Fat: 7 g

Carbs: 64 g

Protein: 10 g

Fiber: 12 g

Pina Colada Smoothie (Vegan

Preparation time: 10 minutes

Ingredients:

- 3 3D squares ice 3D squares, or varying
- 1 banana
- 1 cup new pineapple pieces
- 1/2 cup coconut milk
- 1/2 cup soy milk
- 1 tablespoon agave nectar
- 1 tablespoon ground flax seed
- 1 teaspoon unadulterated vanilla concentrate

Add all fixings to list

Bearings

Blend ice, banana, pineapple, coconut milk, soy milk, agave nectar, flax seed, and vanilla concentrate in a blender until smooth. Empty smoothie into a tall glass.

Sustenance Facts

Nutrition: 586 calories; 29.8 g fat; 78 g carbohydrates;9.7 g protein; 0 mg cholesterol; 84 mg sodium.

Raw Mango Monster Smoothie

Preparation time: 10 minutes

Ingredients:

- 1 tablespoon flax seeds
- 2 tablespoons pepitas (crude pumpkin seeds
- 1 ready mango, cubed
- 1 solidified banana, quartered
- 1/3 cup water, or more to taste
- 3 ice 3D shapes
- 2 leaves kale, or more to taste

Add all fixings to list

Bearings

1. Blend flax seeds in a blender until finely ground; include pepitas and mix until ground, around 1 moment.
2. Place mango, banana, water, ice 3D shapes, and kale in the blender; mix until smooth, kale is completely joined, and the smoothie is uniform in shading, around 3 minutes. Slender with more water to arrive at wanted consistency.

Nutrition: 381 calories; 14.1 g fat; 63 g carbohydrates;9.8 g protein; 0 mg cholesterol; 32

mg sodium.

Vegan Smoothie Bowl With Carrot And Banana

Preparation time: 15 minutes

Ingredients:

- 2 pitted Medjool dates
- 1 solidified banana, cleaved
- 1 cup coarsely cleaved carrot
- 1/2 cup unsweetened vanilla-seasoned almond milk, or more to taste
- 1/2 teaspoon ground cinnamon
- 1/4 teaspoon ground ginger

Topping:

- 2 tablespoons chipped coconut
- 1 tablespoon goji berries
- Add all fixings to list

Bearings

1. Place dates in a little bowl and spread with cold water; let drench, around 5 minutes. Channel and cleave.

2. Place slashed dates, banana, carrot, almond milk, cinnamon, and ginger in a blender; puree until smoothie is thick and smooth. Fill a serving bowl.

3. Top smoothie bowl with chipped coconut and goji berries.

Sustenance Facts

Nutrition: 325 calories; 4.8 g fat; 71.6 g carbohydrates;4.8 g protein; 0 mg cholesterol; 216 mg sodium.

Vanilla Chia Pudding

Preparation time: 15 minutes

Cooking Time: 20 minutes

Ingredients:

- 6 tablespoons chia seeds
- 2 cups almond milk
- 2 tablespoon maple syrup or agave
- 1 teaspoon vanilla concentrate
- 1/2 teaspoon cinnamon

Technique

1. Blend up the almond milk, vanilla, maple syrup, and cinnamon.
2. Pour fluid blend over the chia seeds and mix till seeds are uniformly blended in. Mix again five minutes after the fact, and five minutes after that. Let sit for an hour at any rate, or basically let it sit in the cooler medium-term.

Serve, bested with crisp product of decision. Pudding will keep in the ice chest for as long as four days.

3. 6 tablespoons vegan spread
4. 2/3 cup So Delicious® Dairy Free Hazelnut Coconut Milk Creamer
5. 1/3 cup dull chocolate chips
6. Add all fixings to list

Bearings

1. Preheat stove to 425 degrees F. Line a
   heating sheet with material paper. Filter
   together flour, sugar, preparing powder, salt,
   and heating soft drink in enormous bowl.
   Gather vegan spread and blend into a single
   unit with hands until blend frames enormous,
   coarse morsels the size of peas. Include
   chocolate chips and half and half, blend for a
   couple of more seconds until just dampened.
   Turn the mixture onto a daintily floured work
   surface and press together delicately until the
   batter sticks together in a ball. Pat into a
   hover around 2-inches thick and 6 creeps in
   width.
2. Let sit for 15 minutes at room temperature.
   Cut into 8 wedges. Sprinkle with outstanding
   tablespoon of sugar.
3. Bake for 15-20 minutes or until brilliant on
   top. Permit to cool for a couple of moments,
   before isolating wedges.

Sustenance Facts

Nutrition: 256 calories; 8.9 g fat; 40 g

carbohydrates;3.2 g protein; 0 mg cholesterol; 384 mg sodium.

Orange Pancakes

Preparation time: 10 minutes

Cooking Time: 10 minutes

Ingredients:

- 2 cups white entire wheat flour
- 2 tablespoons heating powder
- 2 tablespoons ground flax meal
- 17 liquid ounces squeezed orange
- 1 teaspoon orange concentrate

Add all fixings to list

Directions:

1. Whisk flour, heating powder, and flax meal together in a bowl; mix squeezed orange and orange concentrate into flour blend until player is well-consolidated.

2. Heat a gently oiled frying pan over medium-high warmth, or an electric iron to 375 degrees F (190 degrees C). Drop hitter by huge spoonfuls onto the frying pan and Cooking Time: until bubbles structure and the edges are dry, 3 to 4 minutes. Flip and Cooking Time: until sautéed on the opposite side, 2 to 3 minutes. Rehash with outstanding

hitter.

Sustenance Facts

Nutrition: 304 calories; 2.7 g fat; 64.6 g carbohydrates;9.6 g protein; 0 mg cholesterol; 734 mg sodium.

Oatmeal Energy Bars

Preparation time: 15 minutes

Cooking Time: 15 minutes

Ingredients:

- 40 min., 24 servings, 91 cals
- 1/3 cups moved oats
- 1/2 cup generally useful flour
- 1/2 cup vegan semi-sweet chocolate chips
- 1/2 cup ground unsalted cashews
- 2 tablespoons shelled unsalted sunflower seeds
- 1 tablespoon ground flax meal
- 1 tablespoon wheat germinutes
- 1/2 teaspoon ground cinnamon
- 1/4 teaspoon ocean salt
- 1/2 cup nectar, warmed
- 1/3 cup almond spread
- 1/2 teaspoon vanilla concentrate

Add all fixings to list

Bearings

1. Preheat stove to 350 degrees F (175 degrees C). Line a 9x11-inch preparing dish with aluminum foil.

2. Whisk oats, flour, chocolate chips, ground cashews, sunflower seeds, flax meal, wheat germin., cinnamon, and ocean salt together in a huge shallow bowl.

3. Stir warmed nectar, almond spread, and vanilla concentrate together in a bowl until well-blended. Empty nectar blend into oat blend; mix until hitter is well-consolidated. Transform hitter out into prepared heating dish. Lay a sheet of waxed paper over player and press solidly to uniformly disseminate in the preparing dish. Expel and dispose of waxed paper.

4. Bake in the preheated stove until brilliant and fragrant, around 12 minutes. Pull aluminum foil from preparing dish and cool bars in the aluminum foil for 10 minutes; evacuate and dispose of aluminum foil. Cut into bars.

Nutrition: 91 calories; 4 g fat; 12.8 g starches; 2 g protein; 0 mg cholesterol; 50 mg sodium.

Lightning Source UK Ltd.
Milton Keynes UK
UKHW020939260221
379431UK00001B/41